"As you explore these poems, you will realize you can trust Agnes Vojta to be your guide. She may lend you her kayak, so you can float an Ozarks river alive with playful otters. Or she will stay with you indoors on a winter day, as you gently turn over the jigsaw pieces of grief With Vojta by your side, you'll learn how to listen carefully for the cry of a kingfisher, how to tend to a tool with tenderness, and how to be wary in a landscape that includes sinkholes and caves. By the twilight of her book, you'll realize that the poet has even tossed you a warm jacket. She has wrapped you in her awareness that our orderly universe—which lets us trace the ellipse of a comet home to its precise star—still allows breathing space for surprise and wonder, for the play of constellations and the random scatter of aster seeds. Vojta's poetry lives between garden and wild river, between honesty and tenderness, between litany and lyricism. Any day I read one of her poems is a good day!"

—Amy Wright Vollmar, author of *Follow: Poems*.

Love Song to Gravity

Poems by Agnes Vojta

Stubborn Mule Press
Devil's Elbow, MO

Copyright © Agnes Vojta, 2025

First Edition: 1 3 5 7 9 10 8 6 4 2

ISBN: 979-8-89975-009-0

LCCN: 2025938476

Cover image: "Secret Message in the Stars" by Greg Edmondson
  (photo by Lisa Halley Melching)

Title page photo: Agnes Vojta

Author photo: Thomas Vojta

Acknowledgemnts

I am deeply grateful to Aliki Barnstone for inviting me into her poetry game circle and to all the writers who create this warm and supportive community. Thanks especially to Lindsey Royce, Deanna Benjamin, Molly McKasson, Elizabeth Bruce, Deborah Gregerman, and Shelly Norris.

Many thanks to Karen Head for her generous encouragement and for all I learned from her.

Thanks to Phil Howerton for inviting me to be part of the Wild Muse collaboration, and to all the other Wild Muse poets. Some poems in this collection were written for that project.

Thanks to Greg Edmondson for permitting me to use his painting Secret Message in the Stars as the cover for this book, and thanks to Lisa Halley Melching for driving through the snow to take the photograph.

And always, thanks to Thomas Vojta for paddling the waters with me.

I thank the editors of the following publications where some of these poems first appeared:

2 River View: "Palimpsest,"
Amethyst Review: "Kelp,"
As It Ought To Be Magazine: "Gone fishing,"
    "The Topography of Grief," "Pope Coffin,"

Black Coffee Review: "We Speak of you,"

Cave Region Review: "After Labor Day," "The River is the Love Song Water Sings to Gravity," "The Old Ferry,"

Flash Boulevard: "Swans and Pelicans," "Paperweights and Nonlinearity,"

Gyroscope Review: "Hourglass,"

I-70 Review: "The Labyrinth and the River," "The Sequel to my Ancestors' Stories,"

Live Nude Poems: "Heartfelt"

Mad Swirl: "Out of Place," "Love Note,"

San Pedro River Review: "Reclamation," "Tell the Bees," "Bonanza Mine,"

Stone Poetry Quarterly: "Eggs,"

Trailerpark Quarterly: "What Remains,"

Wild Muse: Ozarks Nature Poetry: "A Forest of Gramophones," "Any Day you See an Eagle," "Interruption," "Landmarks," "Orange is the Color of Joy," "Stopping by Welch Hospital Ruin",

Young Ravens Literary Review: "Andromeda", "Gravity is Honest"

Contents

On pourrait presque dire que l'eau est folle, à cause de cet hystérique besoin de n'obéir qu'à sa pesanteur, qui la possède comme une idée fixe.

– Francis Ponge

One could almost say that water is mad because of its hysterical need to obey only gravity, which possesses it like a fixed idea.

The River Is the Love Song
Water Sings to Gravity

Follow the current. The trees
bow in reverence, touch
the water like prayers.
The river is the love song
water sings to gravity.

Springs seep from bluffs,
rivulets tickle the stream.
Fern and moss hang heavy,
the hills are a green jungle.
You can lose yourself.

Carry only the necessities.
Notice how little you need.
Ferry only what belongs here.
Thoughts can weigh you down
and make you drown.

Any Day You See an Eagle Is a Good Day

I have lost something I cannot name.
I go to the river and wait.
Perhaps I will find it. Perhaps
I will learn to do without.

I go to the river and wait.
I have nothing to do but to pay attention.
I will learn to do without
the daily clutter and clamor –

there is nothing to do but to pay attention.
Paying attention is a remedy
for the clutter and clamor in my mind.
I watch a snail on a lobelia lip.

Paying attention is an antidote
for apathy and sadness.
I watch the snail on the lobelia lip,
its translucent shell a perfect spiral,

and forget apathy and sadness.
The wood duck leads her ducklings close to shore.
The snail's shell is a translucent spiral.
The ducks weave through the water willows,

led by their mother, close to shore.
An eagle perches on a sycamore.
The ducklings hide between the water willows.
The eagle sits in silence. He unfolds

his wings and lifts off from the sycamore.
I have forgotten what I had lost –
I saw an eagle, unfolded
my grief, found something I cannot name.

The Pope Coffin

I do not know whether dad
believed in heaven.
He had a sense for the sacred.
Sometimes all you see is the fruit;
the root remains secret.

My father never discussed death,
except to say he wanted a coffin
like Pope John Paul II: clear
lines, no frivolous embellishments –
an architect's choice.

The minister spoke about the city-to-come,
solemn and hopeful, consoling
without the saccharine promises
dad would have hated. One must leave
space for uncertainty.

The Topography of Grief

The topography of grief is karst,
riddled with sinkholes
that suddenly open
under your feet, swallow you whole.

I don't know what I expected
to feel. Not this emptiness.
Not nothing. I don't cry
at the sight of my dad's signature.

The letter from probate court
I've been expecting. I know
what it contains: a form letter
and a copy of dad's will.

I cry when I pack his chessboard,
lay the wooden pieces to rest
in their velvet-lined compartments,
close the box, latch the lid.

Don't Ask Why

My father had a sense for beautiful details:
the line of a roof, the feel of a pen in the hand.

On the shore of grief, the coastline is discontinued:
a chasm opens, the way across impossible.

I hoard treasures like a dragon. Mine are invisible,
stuffed inside the hollow of my heart.

My map has a tear that cannot be mended.
A piece is missing. The fragments won't fit together.

I do not believe we meet our ancestors in heaven.
I have no plans for it. Don't ask why.

Swans and Pelicans

The swans sail on the Elbe River, an armada of white, They congregate near the shore where children throw pieces of bread. The swans tolerate the geese and ducks, not too proud to accept the offering. They slowly unfold and fold their angel wings.

The swans are here every year. I have been absent. Forgot the password Homesickness constricts my throat, an incurable ailment. I am here and far away at the same time. You cannot scrub yourself clean of the past.

On the Lake of the Ozarks, pelicans gather to rest on their migration, to replenish with the abundant fish. They perch on narrow logs that lie in the shallows, preentheir plumage with their great beaks, unconcerned by my kayak.

Their nine-feet wingspan is imposing. I watch a squadron fly overhead, their white bodies gleaming in the sun, an undulating ribbon waved by wind, swinging higher and higher, out of sight.

Surrender

At the stream you cannot ford,
you ask for transport.
You must pay the ferryman.
He will name his price.

Through the Unknown, Remembered Gate

The year stumbles towards solstice,
a weary pilgrim who longs to reach
his destination and rest. But the clocks
keep measuring the hours, the bells

cannot be unrung. Earths' rotation –
relentless continuity. We feel time speeding:
the years seem shorter, anniversaries
follow more closely on each other's heels.

Parallels do not intersect in the distance.
All Saints, all Souls. We remember the dead.
Soon it is time to light the candle
for the shortest night and hope we did enough.

Winter Warriors

The day is enveloped in gray.
No snowfall, no white, not even ice —
just a cold that bites bone-deep
and exposes the fault lines.

Fat and content, the orange cat
curls by the window, mesmerized
by the tufted titmouse that pecks
slivers of nuts and seeds at the feeder.

Red grasses shiver in the wind.
Nutshells litter the ground
where lucky squirrels found
food to fill their bellies.

Obscured by leafless bushes,
a brindled body streaks
through the woods, ploughs
through dry leaves. A rustle.

Then nothing. Only the crows'
voices resound in the empty land,
calling to their kin, winter warriors
who roost in the skeletons of sycamores.

February Is a Convincing Liar

Each year, I fall for his false promise
of spring, when he lures me
outside with the first warm days,
and his sunshine beckons: come.

He woos me with his charming smile
and I believe that, this time,
he really means it, and I repress
the memory of cold, grey

weather that always follows
the first warm days.
How can I assume the worst
when he makes me feel wonderful?

He brings me flowers: the first green
tips of daffodils and snowdrops.
He writes songs for me
that robins sing on my lawn.

I am in denial about February.
I should have learned that I cannot
trust him one little bit, but
he is such a convincing liar.

Groundhog Day

February is the longest month.
The world is painted in greyscale. Snow
and sleet cover the roads and the grass.
The groundhog saw his shadow today.

The world is painted in greyscale. Snow
weighs down trees and bushes, heavy and wet.
The groundhog saw his shadow today,
crawled into his den and went back to sleep.

Trees and bushes weighed down, souls, too,
by the monotony of days, the sameness.
I want to crawl in my den and go back to sleep,
drink tea and consume lots of carbs.

The monotony of days, the sameness
stretches the weeks. It is hard to focus.
We drink tea and consume lots of carbs,
dream of sunshine and new beginnings.

Weeks stretch. It is hard to focus until
sleet no longer covers the roads, and the grass
wakes to sunshine and new beginnings –
February is the longest month.

The Patience of Bulbs

I drove home angry. My last
appointment had stood me up.

I had waited, paced, thought of all
I could be doing instead: finishing

my grading, going for a walk
in the sunshine, snuggling my cat.

Finally, I left, resentful
at the wasted time. When I pulled

into my driveway, I spotted green
under the oaks. I brushed

dry leaves aside with my fingers
and uncovered the first snowdrops:

green tips poking through the soil,
white buds swollen with expectation.

They had rested in dark seclusion,
waited until the time was right.

Tell the Bees

I kneel in last year's leaves
to photograph the rue anemones
on their slender stems,
take the same pictures

each year: things deserve
to be honored
every time they emerge,
you once said. I pay homage

to the fiddlehead ferns coiled
tightly with expectation,
the zebra swallowtail who unfolds
his wings in a prayer to spring.

The microbes in the soil are busy
with their invisible work. The earth
did not stop turning
when your heart stopped beating.

Today I folded my arms
around your widow, held her fragile
frame and knew no words
of consolation. And yet –

the trees release clouds of pollen
into a wondrous blue sky.
The white plumes of the blossoms
beckon the bees. Folk wisdom

says one must tell the bees
of a death, hang the hives
with black cloth and sing
to them. I hope someone did.

Palimpsest

Nobody teaches you
how to be a widow.
On your own,
you must learn
a new alphabet,
write the sequel
to your story
on the palimpsest
of your dreams,
scraped of his presence,
cherish the traces
of his hand still
shining through.

After You Left

I have not tended my garden,
have not weeded, not pruned.
Twigs litter the ground
like debris from a broken nest.

Grass swallows
what I wanted to grow.
Only the oregano
flourishes without my help.

I crush some leaves
between my fingers.
They smell of the soup
I do not feel like cooking –

you are not here
to eat it with me.

We Speak of You

as if you are traveling in a far country
and we don't hear from you because
you're having the best time and are too busy
to find a post office or a telephone;

as if we expect you to knock on the door
one Thanksgiving, laden with souvenirs
and stories, and we'll hug you,
set another plate, welcome you home;

as if there wasn't the quiet grave
under the oaks and the headstone
bearing your name.

It Seems Possible

I am distracted
by the unfolding of spring
on this first day of Lent.
Resurrection is in the air.

Green shoots push through soil.
We push aside the unease,
hope we get off without
paying the ransom.

The mourning doves coo
in the cedar where they nested
last year. I unload wood,
stack it in the shed.

Later, I sit in silence, watch
the hawk circle over the field, hear
a flock of geese, too high to see.
It seems possible to bear anything.

Pysanky

The rain left the daffodils bedraggled. The deer ate
　　the plump buds of the tulips.
On the soggy ground, a broken promise of robin
　　song: the blue shell of an egg.

I can reproduce the miracle of yeast each week.
　　Comforting familiar moves.
In a world out of control, I sift flour, measure sugar,
　　slowly separate eggs.

Some thoughts must be handled carefully as if they
　　might crack under your probing.
Set them aside where they're undisturbed. No
　　pressure. They're fragile like blown eggs.

This year, my mind is not on greening. I have not
　　prepared for Easter, have not cut
the hazel branches. I can never find the box with
　　my grandmother's wooden eggs.

Dip the stylus in molten beeswax and write invisible
　　symbols on the shell.
Spells, or silent cries for help. Only after dyeing,
　　they will appear on the egg.

Recipe for mom's Easter bread: divide the dough
    into three strands, braid them.
If you cannot get the ends to join
    seamlessly, hide the flaw under a dyed egg.

Credo

I believe in the resurrection
of green, the miracle
of compost, the mystery
of the seed.

Burial ground turning cradle.

Light bursts every shell open.
No gardener can doubt
the abundance of grace.

Before Dawn

The hills are filled with dreams that drift like mist.
The birds awake and sing their morning prayers.

The irises stand guard, their leaf blades point
towards the sky. Dew-wet, the spiderwort

chooses which flower to unfold today.
Rain heavy, the peonies bow their heads,

their petals folded like origami,
ghostly white lanterns floating in the darkness.

Poetry Reading with
Approaching Storm

We switched off the phones
when they began blaring
weather warnings –
the clouds and the wind

spoke clearly enough:
the sudden rush of cool air,
the ominous darkening
of the sky, the breeze

that picked up papers
and last year's leaves.
We grasped our books tighter,
felt the first sprinkles.

Determined, we held out
until heavy drops splashed
and we rushed, laughing,
inside the old farmhouse.

Settled in the snug room,
with its dark beams and white-
washed walls, we read on,
with the door open

to the drumming of rain
and, later, the frog calls,
and the spring smell
of wet earth.

To Be Tree

To stretch strong arms skyward.
To wear green leaves that can do magic.

To know the spell that transfigures
water and air into sugar.

To shelter and feed woodpeckers and squirrels.
To shade mist flowers that delight bees.

To relinquish all leaves each fall, with equanimity.
To lose branches in winter storms and accept that.

To bear buds each spring that carry instructions
for the great unfolding of green.

To do it again year after year
without question, without giving up.

Cleaning the Tools

Warm sunshine on my skin, the first green buds on the golden currant bush, but there is still ice floating on the bucket under the spigot behind the woodshed. Today's work is finished. I am cleaning the tools: rake, hoe, fork, shovel.

I have scraped the soil off with a wooden spatula. Now I am wiping them with a rag dipped into the bucket. Slowly, like a meditation. I observe how the shovel blade is fixed onto the wooden handle, study the arrow-shape of the hoe, notice how the tines of the fork curve. As I wipe the last traces of dirt away, I thank the tools for their labor. This is prayer.

I pour linseed oil on a woolen rag. I start with the rake head, rub the rag on the tines, between the tines, like drying a child's toes after a bath. I slide the rag up and down the handle, massage the oil into the dried-out wood, lean the rake against the shed. The oil will soak into the wood, preserve it, and make it pleasant to touch.

Now the fork, the hoe, the shovel. I gently oil metal and wood, an act of reverence. The separation between animate and inanimate blurs: the garden is not separate from the tool shed, the rake not separate from my hand. We are one.

When I look closely

Where I no longer mow, the green
stands knee-high: weeds –
a word of judgment I do not like.

I say their names:
white snakeroot, late boneset,
nettle-leaved vervain. I tend

to a patch of mistflower,
cheer it on like a friend:
grow, spread. Even the grass

is no longer a faceless mass.
I know the palm sedge
by its graceful drooping,

the path rush by its inflorescence,
the poverty grass by the curled
whiskers of dried leaves.

Delicate seed heads
in the slight breeze – I kneel
and see the panic grass stir.

Orange Is the Color of Joy

The lilies in the field
do not toil nor spin –
they work the alchemy

of blooming, distill
sunlight, water, and air
into an orange miracle.

In ditches and fencerows
they flower with abandon,
throats open wide. As summer

fades, the lilies tire.
Willpower cannot halt
the wilting of leaves.

The lilies retreat
to their roots, feed
on sugar stores, dream

of blossoms, emerge
in fierce independence
next year. So it is decreed.

Bonanza Mine

Bluffs loom, forbidding.
Water pools, a toxic
shade of turquoise.

Two wooden beams
hold up the roof.
Others rot below.

A heap of rubble, excavated
on the quest for ore.
A rusty pipe. Wreckage

of a claim abandoned.
Caves yawn, dark
tunnels burrow

into the belly of the mine
I don't care to explore.
Let the bats sleep.

The Old Ferry

Like a beached whale,
she lies on the shore,

the motor hangs down
her side like a limp fin,

the brass bell dulled
like a lifeless eye.

The ferryman
has crossed over

the final river.
He is not coming back.

Stopping by Welch Hospital Ruin

Barred window holes,
giraffe rock walls:
field stones, irregular
in shape and size.

Never a tortured place –
just clean moist air,
failing lungs breathing hope
from the cool cave.

The doctor died.
His project crumbled.
Only ghosts now gasp
in the empty shell.

The spring still gushes
from the underground,
choking cold, the water
still rushes to swell the river.

Pioneer Cemetery

The path is overgrown
with river oats and briars.
Few come here.

A row of sandstone slabs,
tinged green by time, tilted
by the weight of decades:

no names, no dates,
no record of lives
faded into history. Only

the oaks stand watch,
and, in the spring, anemones
adorn the ground.

Landmarks

Fog shrouds the river.
Dew collects on leaves,
rolls off in heavy drops.
White asters bloom. The bees

buzz nectar-drunk. Summer
hums a drowsy tune.
Below the calm green spring,
a former mill: a dam,

a rusty turbine – traces
of human work that mar
the landscape. History:
a relay of generations.

The baton itself changes
as it changes hands.

Down by the River

The only sounds: water, kingfishers, wind in the reeds. I dedicate this hour to stillness, let the thoughts that rumble through my brain and threaten my peace drift away like mist.

A heron stalks in the cattails, traces the movement of the fish, waits for the right moment to strike. A family of ducks skirt the water willows, the ducklings copies of one another. Claw prints in the sand, runes that tell a myth from the time before forever.

The last flood left mementos: scarves of leaves and grass draped around tree trunk, logjams piled high at the river bend. The gravel bar where we pitched our tent last year has vanished – a reminder that the only constant is change.

I back up my kayak to withhold some momentum before the passage of swift water that is studded with obstacles. Adrenaline wells up as I navigate through the maze, braced for impact. There will be no winning and no medal, only the exhilaration that I made it through and stayed dry.

River Diary

Barely morning.
Mist swallows all –
blanket of stillness.

Otters gambol,
dive in the waves,
water-sleek fur.

Kingfishers shriek
from bank to bank.
Serene heron.

Campfire smoke
on gravel bar –
incantations.

Signs of beaver:
peeled twigs floating,
tracks up steep banks.

Tall limestone bluffs.
Driftwood for fire.
Sleep on soft sand.

Nightfall. Frogs wake.
Moonlight knits lace
of shadow leaves.

Mild night. Clouds race.
Whippoorwill sings
until daybreak.

Out of Place

If you feel out of place,
let me tell you about the tomato
plant I found growing
on a gravel bar by the river.

A seed from someone's picnic fell,
germinated, and took root
in the sparse dirt the flood
had swept between the pebbles.

The plant is thriving, bears
four ripe tomatoes. I left
them for the critters and for other
wanderers to marvel.

A Forest of Gramophones

The lake is a woodcut,
black and white
wind-carved
zigzag reflections,
the dark silhouette
of the far shore.

In the shallows,
the lotus thrives.
Water beads
on the large round leaves
that float, anchored
to the muddy bottom.

Closer to shore,
the stalks rise higher,
leaves curl
to trumpets, a forest
of gramophones
playing inaudible music –

we only hear
the blue jays shriek
in the distance
and the swish-and-drip
of our paddles.

Reclamation

The weeds have conquered
the train tracks. Fractured
and splintered, the wooden trestle
struggles to span the ravine,

the boundary between past
and present hidden
under tangled briars, twisted
like time's trajectories.

At the old station hotel,
sunlight creeps through the cracks
of boarded windows,
reveals a broken guitar.

The strings have snapped.
They curl like tendrils,
grasp for a song
nobody can hear.

Gone Fishing

A storefront window on Main Street
displays a collection of wooden rainbow
trout. Carved and painted to look real,
their speckled bodies curl in mid-jump

next to a model ship with billowing sails,
an engraved sign reading *Jeremiah Hale,*
Attorney at Law, and a set of scales.
The lights in the office are off.

Perhaps the attorney has gone fishing,
wades knee-deep in the cold river,
hears the kingfishers shriek from bank to bank,
watches silvery fish dance in the reeds.

Perhaps he sits in the dusty backroom
on a desk that is suffocating with papers
and dreams of a ship with white sails
that will come to carry him far away.

To Call this Place *Home*

Triangular patterns of light and shadow on the water. A dragonfly lands on my kayak, stares at me with bulging green eyes, does not move its translucent wings with the black spots. In Chinese culture, dragonflies symbolize change and instability. I want neither.

Next week, I will travel home to see my mother. I will climb the hill and walk through the garden with the old rhododendrons as I have a thousand times. Familiar smells, familiar sights. But Dad won't be there. I wish I were not burdened with the forethought of further grief.

I steer my boat through the water willows onto the bank. Low-hanging branches brush against my shoulders, greenbriar snags my pants as I follow the faint trace up the hill to the old homestead.

Only the chimney still stands, its fieldstone masonry overgrown with vines. Glistening quartz veins adorn the rocks that form the mantel. Nothing else remains of the family who came here to live their dream. Who called this place *home*.

We Call It Gravity

Each summer, I return. I open
the gate and climb the stairs
through the garden to the house.

My steps quicken. I feel the jolt
of coming home, like a comet
that gains momentum as it races

closer. Even at its aphelion,
the comet never loses the memory
of the star, and the star does not release

the comet from its stenciled ellipse.
Why? We call it gravity but cannot
explain why it exists or how it works.

Gravity. Or love.

Tin Pest

Woodpeckers hammer the trunk of the dying
tree. A few struggling branches still
bear leaves. There is no denying
the decay. Bark peels like the crumbling

plaster on the walls. The vines
that curtain the balconies hide
what needs to be repaired.
The patio tiles are cracked.

The water lily in the fountain
unfolds a single flower.
Once it has bloomed, it will sink
to the bottom. The fountain leaks.

In a wicker chest in the attic, I find
my grandfather's violin case.
Horsehair spills from the broken bows.
Nobody has played it in sixty years.

The pewter dishes on the mantel
are spotted with disease: tin pest
eats silver metal into grey powder –
an autocatalytic reaction that, once started,
will only accelerate. No denial can halt it.

A Fractal of Generations

The conifers are taller than the house now.
Whoever planted them did not think
far enough into the future.

I scan my mother's face, search for signs
that should concern me. Quake
at the thought of seeing her changed.

My doll house is still in the attic.
The dolls are lost.
I did not pass them to my daughter.

I see my future in my mother's feet –
the deformed toe joints,
no longer flexible, are my heirloom.

Each spring, mom buys an aquatic plant.
Its floating leaves give birth to miniature copies
of themselves, a fractal of generations.

My mother's hands no longer play the piano.
Sheet music wilts on the shelves.
I hallucinate the sound of sisterly duets.

Do You Remember?

My sister and I toss reminiscences
back and forth like balls flung high
into the air, catch them without effort.

No memories too heavy to be held
in our bare hands. We don't throw
words with sharp edges.

Time has dispersed like smoke
from a bonfire; distance dissolved
like salt in a glass of water.

We watch the recollections soar,
rich stores of moments that were waiting
to be remembered. Our shared past

spans a bridge between then and now,
a solid construction, held up by pillars
that have not crumbled.

What Lies at the Edges of Memory?

I start with the edges and work inward.
Nothing fits together, as if pieces of different
jigsaw puzzles got mixed in one box.

Some memories are stored in trunks locked
with rusty keys. Some are tucked away
in birdhouses and cookie jars.

Each day is a palimpsest, traces of the past
faintly visible. The future is not a blank page.
I cannot white-out my history.

I meander through memories without a compass.
Where the path has a gap, I call
on fantasy to bridge it.

Days have crumbled like ruins
slated for demolition. A few buildings still
stand, inhabited by many moments.

Memories are feral. I cannot entice them to settle.
They skitter away when I come close,
like sandpipers on a beach.

What Remains

The assistant at the Goodwill store recognizes
the old woman who comes in and brings
three pairs of black dress shoes, men's size 10.

She was here last week, dropped off a bag of shirts.
Crisp collars, good quality, they sold quickly.
Another time, two suits. A winter coat, never worn.

The assistant has seen it before. They bring
the dress clothes first. Later, the sweatpants
and the everyday jackets. They hesitate

when they hand over the first small bundle.
Then they grow bolder, and the bags get larger.
Until they don't come anymore.

He knows they keep the faded favorites
longest: the grey sweater with the frayed seam,
the worn slippers. They are not fit to donate anyway.

Interruption

The birds scatter.
A large-winged shadow
swoops –

settles on the dead
branch above the feeder.
The haw surveys the field.

When he flies off, the branch
bounces up and down –
long after he is gone

and the chickadees are already back,
chirping and chattering
as if nothing happened.

O that we may so regroup after peril,
return again and again
to our ordinary lives.

Heart Felt

I put the laundry in the dryer
and remember the day we strolled
through the town after lunch,
not ready to say goodbye.

The years of absence
had fallen away like dust
in a breeze. Confidences
came easy. We wandered

into a store that sold soaps
and wooden brushes. A glass jar
with felted dryer balls
stood on the windowsill. I told you

how the dogs had claimed
my old one as a toy. You picked
a ball with a rainbow heart
and bought it for me.

I watched your car disappear
down the road. We forgot
to take a picture. But I smile
and think of you when I open my dryer.

Andromeda

Two and a half million light-years
away, she spins, joyful
in her obedience to gravity.

Her spiral arms trail veils
of dust, as if a whirlwind dances
with a nebula of stars.

She scatters luminous clouds,
circles with the grace of a princess,
with the violence of a hurricane.

Young stars fall from her arms,
glow brightly, diminish to ghosts.
We cannot discern what is at her center.

Alchemy

Lay the tarnished silver
on a piece of aluminum foil
in a glass bowl, sprinkle
a spoonful of salt, pour
boiling water over it, wait.

You do not need technical terms
like anode and cathode. You do not need
to know the chemistry, why sulfur feels
a stronger affinity to aluminum and leaves
the silver shiny. You can marvel at the magic.

I perform the trick in my kitchen.
A faint sulfuric odor rises,
the silver spiral with the turquoise
center I bought from a Navajo artisan
in Santa Fe looks like new.

If only we could cure the ills
of the world with such simple potions,
release what tarnishes souls
in a foul-smelling whiff
at the wave of a wand.

Swarm Dynamics

My physicist friend models
the swarm dynamics of birds.
He solves differential equations,
speaks of *statistical field theory*
and *marginal speed confinement.*
His paper appeared
in a prestigious journal.

I watch the murmuration,
hundreds of starlings swirling
in perfect synchronicity. They know
where to be at each moment,
how to adjust their flight
to their neighbors, how to trust
each wingbeat. I am glad they do.

Newton's Cat or:
My Lectures Are Not Outdated

My ears ring with the erratic demands
that define *ridiculous*. I am inclined
to decline further assignments.
I want to resign. Sick of leaning in, I recline

and fantasize about operatic tantrums
I will not throw because I am sane enough to know
that to show my irritation would change nothing.
Instead, I throw on a sweater and head outside.

I wield the hedge trimmer like a sword,
slash at arborvitae and yew, pile branches high
on the wheelbarrow; much depends on it,
that trusty conveyance of refuse to the compost.

I rage against the machine and the puppet masters
before dutifully resuming the tedious task
of updating information that is neither expired
nor outdated – just published a while ago.

Oh, the curse of the internet where longevity
is a flaw, and everything must be new and shiny
and in fashion, dresses as well as ideas,
but Sir Isaac has been dead three hundred years,

and boxes still slide down inclines, and jumping cats
still follow parabolic trajectories, if they are not
resting on a bed or a chair in which case the net force
they feel is still zero, just as it was three hundred years

ago when Newton's cat laid himself down
on the paper Newton was writing on
because cats were the same back then, too,
and nothing about their behavior requires updating.

Paperweights and Nonlinearity

Air bubbles trapped in the glass paperweight – patterns like ink drops dispersing in water. The light, refracted by the different layers, shimmers them in shades of green. In the center a dark circle, like a kernel of wisdom. I do not need it to weigh down papers. My papers are ordered, filed away. I just like looking at it, like moving the smooth shape in my hand like a worry stone.

I untangle the knots of the necklace I found in my jewelry box. With the tips of my fingers, I wiggle the gold links, work from the ends towards the middle, solve the riddle, resurrect the chain to its linear form. I am addicted to order.

There is order in chaos. The patterns inside the paperweight only appear random. They formed during cooling, a process governed by nonlinear dynamics. Nonlinearity leads to complex structures that are as varied as living things. My linear brain can work out that math.

Love Note

My husband does not bring me roses.
He does not surprise me
with candlelight dinners
on our anniversary.

While I was at a poetry reading last night,
he sharpened the kitchen knives
and left a note in the drawer:
"Caution! Sharp!"

Kelp

Fog creeps in from the sea.
Seven pelicans sail overhead;
silhouettes in the mist.
I find a stone with a keyhole.

The beach is littered with kelp.
Translucent blades, criss-crossed with ridges.
Firm airbladders. The holdfast grips
a rock with many fingers.

The kelp whispers questions:
What lifts you up? What do you cling to?
How do you find balance
between holding on and floating away?

As If

Sand runs smoothly through the hourglass
as if time flows linearly,
undisturbed by turbulence;

as if each day isn't a sequence
of ripples and eddies, swirling
water and calm pools;

as if some days aren't class V rapids
that leave no space for breath and smash you
into obstacles you didn't have time to notice;

as if you aren't abandoned
to the waves that could suddenly crater
and swallow you;

as if the days are crystal water
that reflects blue sky, and the egret
stalks the shore of the hours, poised and patient;

as if you can dive and open your eyes
underwater and clearly see the fish;

as if you can abide and drift.

Finally, Rain

The water beads my windowpane. I look
out to the garden, wasted by the drought
and the speckled fawns who, desperate for green,
have gnawed my cucumber plants to the ground
and nibbled the tomatoes. Only the herbs
remain unscathed, protected by their fragrance.

Finally, rain, reviving wilted leaves,
softening the brown stubble of the lawn.
Roots wake and plunge deep on their quest for moisture,
claw their way through the clay to the precious drops.
The empty creek bed fills, the current rushes
over slick limestone through the small canyon.

Up on a branch, a flicker fledgling howls
until his mother stuffs his beak with insects.
Over and over, they enact the ritual
of feeding. Seven crows make a racket
in the sycamore. Robins pick mulberries,
red and purple like gemstones.

After Labor Day

The tourists have departed
with their boom boxes and coolers,
left behind beer cans,
sunscreen bottles, and silence.

The boys who stacked boats all summer
have gone back to school,
tanned, with broader shoulders,
a season closer to manhood.

The girl who sold smiles and ice cream
has gone, too, with her memory
of kissing a boy with sun-bleached hair
one evening down by the river.

The blue rafts are deflated and packed away.
A lone canoe is lying on the landing,
like an old turtle who has seen much
and knows how to survive through winter.

Gravity Is Honest

As days grow shorter
and nights cooler,
a surge of energy rushes
through the garden:

grass blades stretch,
moisture shoots into the tips
of the tomato leaves.
The basil goes to seed.

In parting, summer pushes
the last fruit towards ripening.
Fall as a metaphor for aging?
That has been done before;

there's nothing that hasn't
been said. Trees shed leaves.
Water trickles downhill.
Gravity is honest.

Because Earth's axis tilts,
we get less sunlight. That's all.
Seasons don't happen
for our spiritual insight

but by accident: a cosmic
collision knocked Earth off-kilter.
It also created the moon.
We can seek a metaphor

in that, too. Or just observe
the forces that make galaxies
spiral and black holes coalesce.
And marvel that we exist at all.

Plum Cake for Dad

Dad, I baked a plum cake today.
It's what you always want for your birthday.
September is plum month. The cake is legend
among your friends.
The proper plums are small and blue.
The purple ones from the supermarket
don't have the flavor, but they'll have to do.
You'd scorn the American butter.
I bought the Irish butter so the streusel
will be rich enough for your liking.
I don't bake this cake often. It won't taste
like grandma's or like mom's. It's the best
approximation I can manage.
I can't send you flowers this year. Nobody
can take them to the cemetery for me.
So I'll eat a piece of cake in your memory.
I know you would approve.

Wait for the Wind

I am restless, a tumbleweed driven by the wind.
On empty desert highways all you hear is the wind.

Lay a mandala of leaves: orange, yellow, and red.
Construct the pattern carefully, then wait for the wind.

Rain warped the keys of the piano on La Cumbre peak.
I hear the ponderosa pines rustle in the wind.

Twilight falls. The hours have dwindled like a dying fire.
The embers burned. The last candle flickers in the wind.

Petrichor, the smell of air after a summer rain.
I don't know the word for the scent of snow on the wind.

Hourglass

The shadows on the sundials lengthen. Daylight
   leaks from the year.
The balance tilts to darkness. We tally the accounts
   of the year.

The trees acknowledge the season with the yellowing
   of their leaves.
Scent of impermanence on the wind. We sense the
   end of the year.

Bees mingle in the mint, tumble in the goldenrod.
   Last harvest.
Tenaciously, the leaves cling to the branches. We
   cling to the years.

Old wives' summer: golden days that smell of apples
   and wilting leaves.
My aged cat still sunned herself at my feet this time
   last year.

Leaves sail on the breeze, land on the water and float
   down the river.
They are teaching lessons about letting go, I think
   every year.

Seeds fall, a raft to carry blueprints of life across the
   winter.
The promise lies patiently. The spring showers will
   wake it next year.

We try to row but we cannot steer, cannot decipher
   the map.
The sand in the hourglass remains hidden. How
   many more years?

For my father's birthday, I send flowers to cheer up
   my mother.
She ordered a bench to sit by his grave. Soon it will
   be a year.

To Every Thing There Is a Season

The evening before the first freeze,
I harvest the last of the basil.
The wind is blowing the leaves
off the oaks, the days will fade
from gold to grey. The asters
have finished blooming, their seeds
ripe to float away – endings
that become beginnings.

Last year, I coaxed the basil plant
over the winter on my windowsill.
It died in February. I won't try
again. Tomorrow, its leaves
will be shriveled and black. I cut
the last tomatoes for a salad, slice
basil into thin ribbons: a feast
to bid goodbye to summer. I'll embrace

the season of pumpkins, root
vegetables, and cabbage, wait,
until it is summer again and the basil
grows lush and green, and the farmer
brings her first crop of sun-warm
tomatoes to the market, sweeter
from the anticipation, more flavorful
because we did without.

In the Last Hour of Precious Light

The swallows muster
for their big undertaking.
Prescient of coming winter,
adamant to leave
before the storms,
their mission is migration.

The robins gather by the creek,
fill the air with shrieks,
their bodies streak
like arrows across the sky
that is still blue
in the last hour of precious light.

A low sunbeam gilds
the path, illuminates
wilted leaves and white asters
nobody planted – they happened,
from a surplus of seeds
carried on a breeze like a kiss.

See, They Depart, and We Go with Them

The heat broke, and a steady rain fell gently
to rescue fields and forests from the drought.
I can't remember the last time the sky
was grey, the light was dim and cozy –
time to retreat indoors, drink tea, bake bread,
light the first candle of the season.

We are past equinox, and nightfall
comes early, morning light wakes later.
The autumn air is haunted with goodbyes
and memories of goodbyes that mark, like cairns,
a path across a wide uncharted realm.
My kin who walked before me left no footsteps –

just memories that float like lanterns
and calmly light my way.

The Labyrinth and the River

Paddle the water before you. You cannot go back
    upriver.
Lean towards the obstacle. These are your lessons
    from the river.

The hummingbird moth hovers over the evening
    primrose.
White flowers, white noise of the rapids, white song
    of the river.

Go to the woods. See: the sky has laid itself onto
    the ground.
A pilgrimage. The miracle of bluebells by the river.

Two owls hoot in the trees. Their voices resonate in
    the grove.
Owl calls in the moonlight. How do I deserve this
    grace, River?

Let peace cocoon you. Guilt has no power, sin is a
    construct.
Only judge what disfigures a soul. This, whispers
    the river.

Barefoot, I let the labyrinth carry me to the center.
There is no difference between the labyrinth and
    the river.

The Sequel to My Ancestors' Stories.

On Saturdays, the widows walk in the graveyards.
The flowers on the graves wilted for lack of rain.

Light a candle and place it before the icon.
Kneel on the tiles, pray for solace, patience, and rain.

In the closet, the old red dress with the torn hem.
Two broken umbrellas that don't hold back the rain.

Long ago, my mom used to play the piano.
Notes fell in arpeggios like distant drops of rain.

I am the sequel to my ancestors' stories.
To their nimbus clouds in the sky, I am the rain.

Notes

Through the Unknown, Remembered Gate: The title is a line from T.S. Eliot's Four Quartets.

Pysanky: Pysanky are eggs decorated with a wax-resist method. The name comes from the Ukrainian word pysaty, "to write". The designs are written on the egg in hot wax before it is placed in the dye.

Orange is the Color of Joy: Matthew 6:28: "Consider the lilies of the field, how they grow; they toil not, neither do they spin."

To Call This Place Home: "forethought of further grief" references "I come into the peace of wild things who do not tax their lives with forethought of grief" from Wendell Berry's poem The Peace of Wild Things.

To Every Thing There Is a Season: Ecclesiastes 3:1

The Labyrinth and the River: "Only judge what disfigures the soul": in Frank Herbert's Dune, "Thou shalt not disfigure the soul" is the supreme commandment in the Orange Catholic Bible, the fictitious holy book.

See, They Depart, and We Go with Them: The title is a line from T.S. Eliot's Four Quartets.

Agnes Vojta grew up in Germany and now lives in Rolla, Missouri where she teaches physics at Missouri S&T and hikes the Ozarks. She is the author of *Porous Land, The Eden of Perhaps,* and *A Coracle for Dreams* (Spartan Press) and of a chapter in Wild Muse: *Ozarks Nature Poetry* (Cornerpost Press, 2022.) Agnes is associate editor of *Thimble Literary Magazine* and host of the Poetry at the Pub reading series in Rolla. Her poems have appeared in a variety of magazines; you can read some of them on her website agnesvojta.com.

This project was made possible, in part, by generous support from the Osage Arts Community.

Osage Arts Community provides temporary time, space and support for the creation of new artistic works in a retreat format, serving creative people of all kinds — visual artists, composers, poets, fiction and nonfiction writers. Located on a 152-acre farm in an isolated rural mountainside setting in Central Missouri and bordered by ¾ of a mile of the Gasconade River, OAC provides residencies to those working alone, as well as welcoming collaborative teams, offering living space and workspace in a country environment to emerging and mid-career artists. For more information, visit us at www.osageac.org

Osage Arts Community

www.ingramcontent.com/pod-product-compliance
Lightning Source LLC
Chambersburg PA
CBHW020758130626
46554CB00006B/2256